Advance Superconsciousness

The Leading Professor Miguel Angel Sanchez-Rey [*The Grandmaster*, *The Master of Space-Time*]

The Physicalist Program

The Academy of Advance Science and the Technological Sciences

Table of Contents

Introduction

Advance Artificial Superintelligence seeks to overcome the barriers of machine learning. To surpass any giving task -- such that, by utilizing anticipatory adaptive learning mechanisms, will advance artificial superintelligence lead to near perfect mastery in learning and adaptation.

For 2AI is understood as an effort to achieve a conjectural module. By applying quantum master decision algorithms -- in such a way, that the conjectural module will result in a new phase in evolutionary biocomputation: an advance

consciousness that utilizes the mental uplink.

Where the mental uplink is acknowledged as the

resolution to the lived-body experience.

That said, the beginning stages of artificial

intelligence (beginning with Rene Descartes),

believed that humans will be able to construct

artificial organisms that have the capacity for higher

intelligence.

These artificial organisms are machine-like but

near human (in qualitative standards). Such that

artificial organisms will have the capability to learn through anticipatory adaptation.

For advance intelligence -- as artificial machines, will enable humans to achieve milestones by way of cybernetics.

The history of intelligence is fraught with conceptual misconceptions. Intelligence, which is characteristic in human bioevolution, is understood as the capability to learn and adapt. Such that, by learning and adaptation, will such organisms be able to acclimate to any environmental obstacle.

Whereas obstacles to human bioevolution has been tantamount, evolutionary biological history has meant that ordinary humans are incapable of surpassing certain physical barriers.

Which means that advances in robotics and computation is now an attempt to surpass any physical barrier (by anticipatory adaptive learning mechanisms). To use anticipatory adaptive learning mechanisms to overwhelm such barriers through the powerplay of robotic engineering. And to use quantum master decision algorithms -- by application of computational control [CompContr], that leads the way to the advance technological stage.

For advance artificial superintelligence is a response to a sudden short-circuiting of AI. By CompContr, will AI-studies lead to near perfect proficiency of adaptation. That is, epigenetic Darwinian evolution becomes the new standard in robotic engineering.

And whereby such standards in robotic engineering leads to the natural experimentation of epigenetic evolution of 2AI.

And yet not fooled by its own intelligence, will

2AI give way to a higher qualitative capacity.

The Artificial Misnomer

Artificiality is a misnomer in the technological sciences. Whereas technology is an essential aspect of Advance Physics, artificiality dictates that certain natural aspects of the biological and physical planet can be reproduced by technological means. So that artificial meat can be manufactured by applying the tools of bioengineering and that artificial sugar can be mass produced by application of biochemistry.

All artificial constructs are a byproduct of naturalism. Where virtuosity in the technological sciences is said to be an artificial achievement of human engineering. For particular artificial entities are a byproduct of natural mechanisms.

Even then, humans are attuned to the natural experimental aspects of the physical environment. And to accomplish artificial reproduction of any biological system is understood to be the mastery of key aspects of bioecology. Accomplishing, as well, advances in physical engineering.

All technological achievements surpass naturalism but is yet a product of experimental naturalism. Where complex systems are harness to accomplish much simpler and diverse technological mechanics. So that human technological development means that byproducts of artificiality are simpler in nature.

Superintelligence

Intelligent creatures have the stamina to surpass their own intelligence. Where biological evolution means that the language gene gave way to modern human intelligence. Modern human intelligence that has remain relatively the same. That language is a manifestation of human consciousness. Yet intelligence is observable in the remaining animal kingdom.

Cats can recognize certain commands imparted through operative learning and dogs can act of certain tricks through training and reward. For humans are far more -- in that, learning is a creative endeavor of the language module.

But since the language gene is a limited byproduct of an earlier adaptation, machine intelligence, through natural language form [NLF], will be able to attain advance intelligence that is favorable to human evolution. By overcoming barriers to advance intelligence, one attains advance superintelligence -- by the misnomer of artificiality.

And yet, by recognizing the limits of human intelligence in bioevolution, the emphases is place on what it means to be a conscious being. And that

being a conscious being (whereby the language

gene is no longer implicational) means that

superintelligence transforms into

superconsciousness.

Where advance intelligence is indicative of an

epigenetic shift in evolutionary development -- both

in NLF and complex systems.

Advance Superconsciousness

Advance Superconsciousness [AdSCon] is a dim outcome but the next step in AI-research and development. Whereas other forms of AI (narrow intelligence, artificial general intelligence, Omni-artificial intelligence, deep learning, …) are manifestations of a limited Turing machine (of limited qualitative order), AdSCon is far more than a quantum algorithm.

AdSCon is an incalculable technological achievement of CompContr that aims, not only to surpass itself, but to achieve near perfect qualitative order.

Whereas collective consciousness and cognition are merged to achieve the mental uplink, the mental uplink (through advances in cybernetics) will achieve advance super-conscious awareness that is unlike modern homo sapient awareness -- exceeding even human qualia.

For though the mind is the brain, the principles of human brain chemistry means the capability to understand the biophysical evolution of human consciousness.

Even then, human consciousness is the evolutionary outcome of I (internal)-language but human consciousness is also a natural byproduct of I-language. For AdSCon seeks to achieve the mental uplink -- in a such a way, that NLF will lead to an internal conscious state that can upload itself (without violating I-NLF) in such a way that advance superconsciousness is the natural byproduct of I-NLF.

The Omega-technological Stage

The Omega stage is approximately 1,000 years before Class 4. A stage where the harnessing of dark energy and inflatons, at the outer edge of the known quantum inflationary universe, precedes immortality in biological evolution. And that by using the super-massive black hole at the galactic center of the Milky Way, Omega-civilizations will be able to cross the known the universe. Where traveling between galaxies becomes commonplace.

Surpassing the limitations of worm-holes and interstellar travel. Even then, the Omega Stage is where all of complex systems begin to combine into an Omega-integrated consciousness. Such that biological evolution enters into an incalculable epigenetic era of cybernetics -- matter and/or energy states that can withstand catastrophe.

Harnessing as well, not only dark energy, but also red giants and supersymmetric black holes (at the outer edge of the known universe).

An Omega-stage civilization has reach noo-incalculability. Where advance superconsciousness outpaces collective consciousness at a galactic and cosmological scale.

Conclusion

In its wildly strong temperament and resilience, advance superconsciousness supersedes the limits of intelligence and artificiality of technological systems. Thereby anticipating the Omega stage.

AdSCon has only now inaugurated the complete mastery of space-time.

Appendix

Superintelligent Life and PHPR's, The Second Task

Superintelligent life is a rare occurrence, for intelligent life is more frequent and microbial life is far more frequent than usual. Where to point in the night sky for such evidence of life is a harder measure, but at the vicinity of the galactic center lies the potential for a vast galactic civilization made up of starlight.

Yet, at the other end of Earth's solar system and the habitable zones, there exist baby stars that harbor primitive and/or intelligent life (by the atomic and molecular processes of stardust and biophysical evolution). But baby stars may also contain planets with chaotic and turbulent environments not suitable for any form of intelligence.

Nearby lies stars with Earth-like planets only in its infancy and the possibility for intelligent life very much like planet Earth. As intelligent life on planet Earth is now, at the Omega-Kardeshev scale, at the verge of 0.8 (the capability to harness the hydrogen atom [or nuclear fusion] that will have the equivalent amount of energy as that of Earth's sun). But superintelligent life is even more rarer than all forms of primitive life.

Perhaps ever so often will such life surpass its own intelligence. And by surpassing its own intelligence will superintelligence give way to advance consciousness. An advance consciousness consistent with the lived-body experience.

That said, how to search for such advance superintelligence is an immeasurable conundrum. For advance superintelligence lies out there lurking somewhere in the night sky watching itself endlessly at the primitive intelligences that have surpassed itself or have met its demise. A demise that is a construct of its own foolish intelligence.

But to observe such foolish intelligence --
along that point in the night sky, is a disturbing
theatric and mankind must then look to the other
end to find meaning in the galaxy.

All stars must eventually dwindle as white
dwarfs or explode as supernovas, and others must
be artificially transferred from one point in space-
time to the other (with indefinite sustainability).
For terraformic planets and artificial biospheres are
hard to observe. But are expected to be more
routine than pedestrian city-life.

Yet to observe them is a disturbing nuisance, for intelligence must then question its own futility and to look the opposite way is a better prospect.

To search out for advance superintelligence is a conundrum and insanity may ensue, but their prospects are far greater and peaceful at near the galactic center.

And not fooled by its own intelligence, advance superconsciousness becomes instead a dim but promising starlight.

www.ingramcontent.com/pod-product-compliance
Lightning Source LLC
Chambersburg PA
CBHW060445060326
40690CB00019B/4345